TALES OF BLACK FISH BEAR

Black Fish Bear and Me!

DEDICATED TO:

The teachers of our children.

For information regarding permission, write to:
BLACK FISH PUBLISHING,
a division of **BLACK FISH TRADING CO.**
P.O. Box 1133
East Orleans, MA 02643-1133

Black Fish Trading Co.

 Published by Black Fish Publishing.
Computer graphics by Linda A. Quinlan
Printed in Korea

This is Black Fish Bear!

This is Me! My name is ______________________________

Make a picture of yourself.
This is called a **self-portrait**.

Black Fish Bear lives in the Enchanted Forest near Black Fish Creek. His home is called a **den**.

I live here. My home is called ____________________

Mother Earth's creatures live in many different kinds of homes! Linda Bird lives in a nest. Wendy Woodchuck and Sniffles the Skunk live in **burrows**. Wise Old Whale lives in the ocean and Pammy Duck lives in a **marsh**. Make a picture of your home.

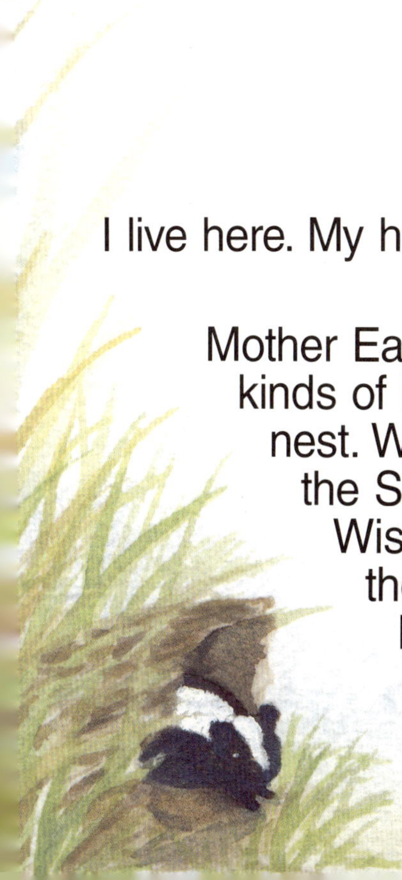

Black Fish Bear lives with Mother Earth, Father Sky, Grandmother Moon and Grandfather Sun. They are all part of his family.

I live with ____

____

They are part of my family. Families have many different names. A family of whales is called a **pod**. A family of birds is called a **flock**. A family of geese is called a **gaggle**. A family of fish is called a **school**. Make a picture of your family.

Black Fish Bear's friends are Ridley Turtle, Scilla Seal, Gwenny Gull, Wise Old Whale, Linda Bird, Red Tailed Hawk, Albert the Butterfly, Sniffles the Skunk, Pammy Duck, Wendy Woodchuck and Stingy Squirrel.

My friends are ______________________________

____

____

Always check with your parents before you go out to play with your friends. From some of our adventures with Black Fish Bear we have learned that friends help each other. It's also important to say no to your friends if they want to do something that you know is not safe. Friends help each other to make good choices! Make a picture of something you like to do with your friends.

When Black Fish Bear plays with his friends they do many different things! Black Fish Bear swims in the bay with Wise Old Whale and climbs trees in the Enchanted Forest with Stingy Squirrel.

When I play with my friends we like to

Like Black Fish Bear, your friends may enjoy doing many different things. Make a picture of something you and your friends like to do.

When Black Fish Bear is happy he likes to run through the Enchanted Forest as fast as he can with his good friend Pammy Duck!

When I'm happy I like to ____

____

There are many ways to show happy feelings! Smiling, laughing, playing and sharing are some of the ways that show us when our friends are happy. Make a picture of something you do when you're happy!

When Black Fish Bear is sad he talks to Wise Old Whale. Wise Old Whale is a good listener and for some reason Black Fish Bear always feels better after sharing his feelings with a trusted friend.

When I am sad I talk to ______________________________

Everyone is sad sometimes. When you're happy or sad, it's important to share your feelings with someone special. Make a picture of someone you like to be with when you're sad.

Black Fish Bear is good at climbing trees!
Wise Old Whale can't climb trees, but he is a
terrific swimmer!

I am good at ______________________________

Everyone is good at something!
Make a picture of something that you do well.

Some things are difficult for Black Fish Bear. He can't fly like Pammy Duck or jump from tree to tree as well as Stingy Squirrel.

_______________________________ is difficult for me.

Usually, we don't like to do things which are difficult. However, most new things are not easy, especially at first. Sometimes by trying a different way, practicing or with the help of friends, we can make difficult things easier. Make a picture of something that is not easy for you.

Black Fish Bear wants to learn about
and understand everything!

Why do leaves change colors?
What is a rainbow?
How do caterpillars change into butterflies?
What makes the tides change?

I want to learn about ______________________________

____

____

Mother Earth is full of **mysteries**. Exploring, **investigating**, listening, asking questions, thinking, **predicting**, and reading are some of the ways you can learn more about your world.

Make a picture of something you want to know more about.

Someday Black Fish Bear would like to visit other places on Mother Earth. There are places which are very different from the Enchanted Forest! Some places are very, very hot... very, very cold... or very, very **humid** and rainy all year long!

Someday, I would like to visit ______________________________

Visiting other places is always a new adventure! We can make new friends, try new things and discover new ideas!
Create a picture of a place you would like to visit.

Lessons

❖ All of our homes and families are different.

❖ Our homes and families may have different names.

❖ Always check with your parents before you go out to play with your friends.

❖ It's important to say NO to your friends if they want to do something which you know is not safe.

❖ Friends help each other to make good choices.

❖ Everyone feels sad sometimes.

❖ There are many different ways to show our feelings.

❖ We usually feel better after we share our feelings with a trusted friend.

❖ Everyone is different and everyone can do something well.

❖ By trying a different way, practicing or with the help of a friend, we can make difficult things easier.

❖ It is fun to learn about our world.

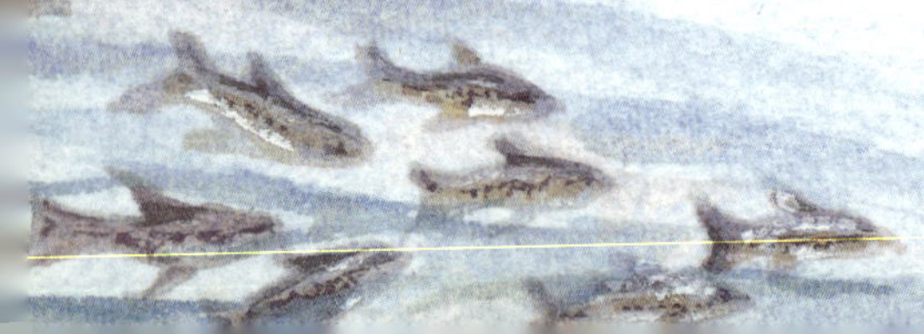

Vocabulary

Self-portrait
Den
Nest
Burrow
Marsh
Pod
Flock
Gaggle
School
Mystery
Investigate
Predict
Humid

The Adventures Continue....

Tales of Black Fish Bear

Mystery of the Tides
Winter at Black Fish Creek
Spring on Butterfly Hill
Autumn in the Enchanted Forest
Summer on Black Fish Bay

Write to Black Fish Bear and he will write back!!

(your mailing address here)

Dear Black Fish Bear,

From,

BLACK FISH BEAR

Black Fish Trading Co.
PO Box 1133
East Orleans, MA 02643-1133